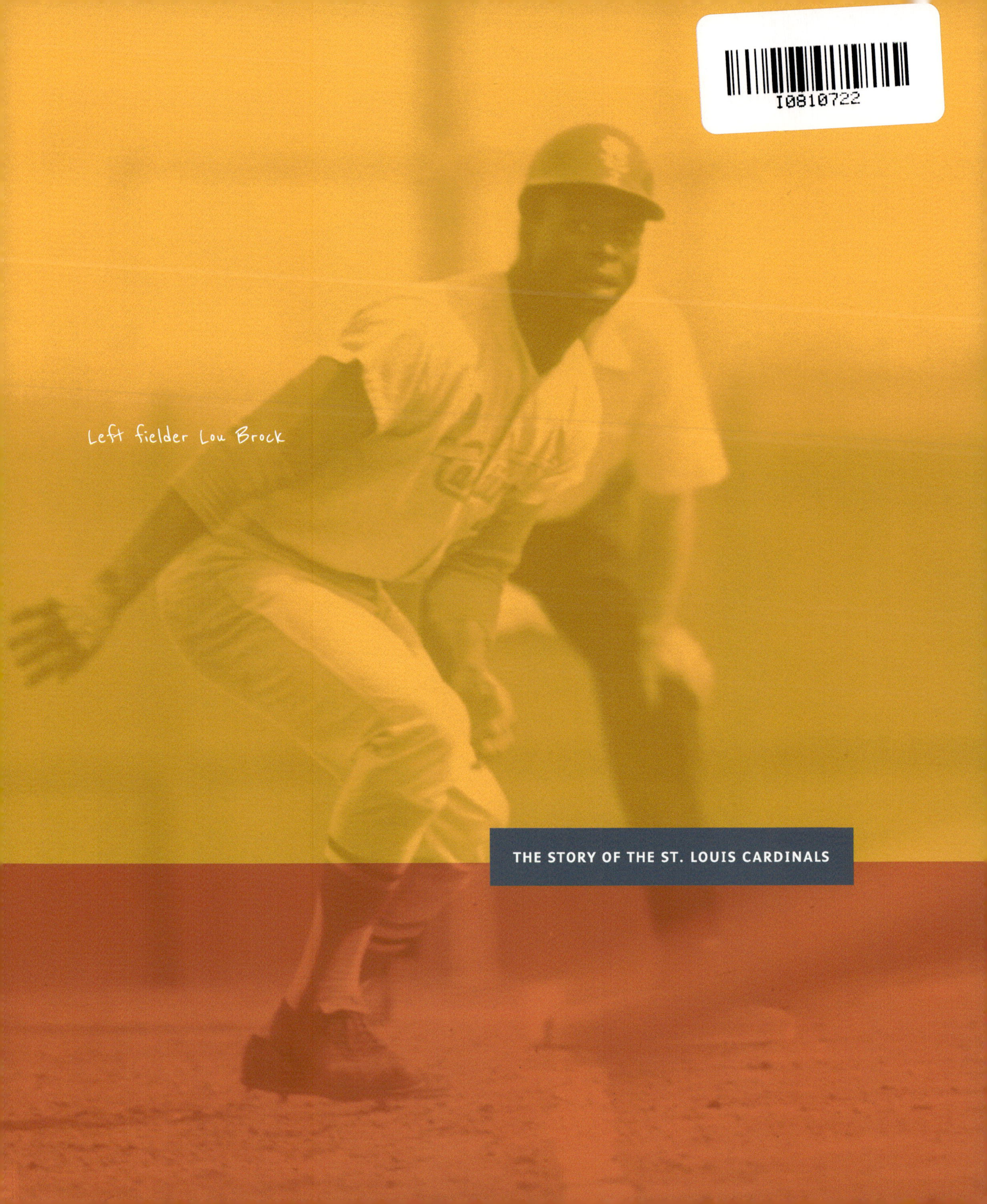

Left fielder Lou Brock

THE STORY OF THE ST. LOUIS CARDINALS

Third baseman Nolan Arenado

THE STORY OF THE

ST. LOUIS CARDINALS

JOE TISCHLER

Pitcher Chris Carpenter

CREATIVE SPORTS

CREATIVE EDUCATION / CREATIVE PAPERBACKS

Published by Creative Education and Creative Paperbacks
P.O. Box 227, Mankato, Minnesota 56002
Creative Education and Creative Paperbacks are imprints of
The Creative Company
www.thecreativecompany.us

Book Design by Wyeth Morgan
Art direction by Blue Design (www.bluedes.com)

Images by Alamy Stock Photo/Bill Greenblatt, 4-5, 32; Associated Press/Jeff Chiu, cover; Dreamstime/F11photo, 11; Getty Images/Al Tielemans, 7 (bottom, left), 10, 29, Ali Overstreet, 31, B Bennett, cover, 15, Bernstein Associates, 7 (top, right), Bettmann, 6 (bottom, right), Dilip Vishwanat, 2, Elsa, 6 (top, right), 7 (top, left), Focus On Sport, 6 (bottom, left), 22-23, FPG, 12, G Fiume, 7 (bottom, right), Hulton Archive, 20, John Biever, 10, Kyle Rivas, 30, Louis Requena, 6 (top, left), Otto Greule Jr, 25, Photo File, 1, 16, Rich Pilling/Sporting News, 26-27, Rob Leiter, 3, Ron T. Ennis/Fort Worth Star-Telegram, 9, Ron Vesely, 19, Transcendental Graphics, 18

Library of Congress Cataloging-in-Publication Data
Names: Tischler, Joe author
Title: The story of the St. Louis Cardinals / Joe Tischler.
Description: Mankato, Minnesota : Creative Education and Creative Paperbacks, [2026] | Series: Creative sports: Major League Baseball | Includes index. | Audience: Ages 8-12 | Audience: Grades 4-6 | Summary: "Discover the St. Louis Cardinals' thrilling journey from their origins in 1882 to recent seasons, featuring legendary players, historic moments, and the Major League Baseball team's loyal fanbase. Written for middle-grade readers. Includes table of contents, sidebars, and index"– Provided by publisher.
Identifiers: LCCN 2025019588 (print) | LCCN 2025019589 (ebook) | ISBN 9798895811092 library binding | ISBN 9798896800620 paperback | ISBN 9798895812358 ebook
Subjects: LCSH: St. Louis Cardinals (Baseball team)–Juvenile literature | Baseball teams–United States–History–Juvenile literature | Major League Baseball (Organization)–Juvenile literature
Classification: LCC GV875.S74 T57 2026 (print) | LCC GV875.S74 (ebook) | DDC 796.357/640977866–dc23/eng/20250621
LC record available at https://lccn.loc.gov/2025019588
LC ebook record available at https://lccn.loc.gov/2025019589

Printed in the United States

Second baseman Kolten Wong

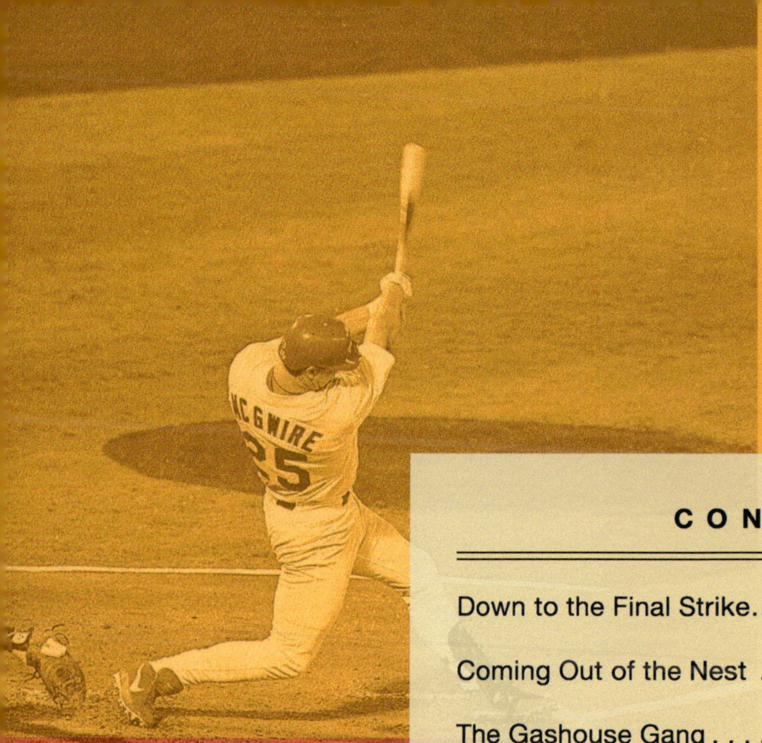

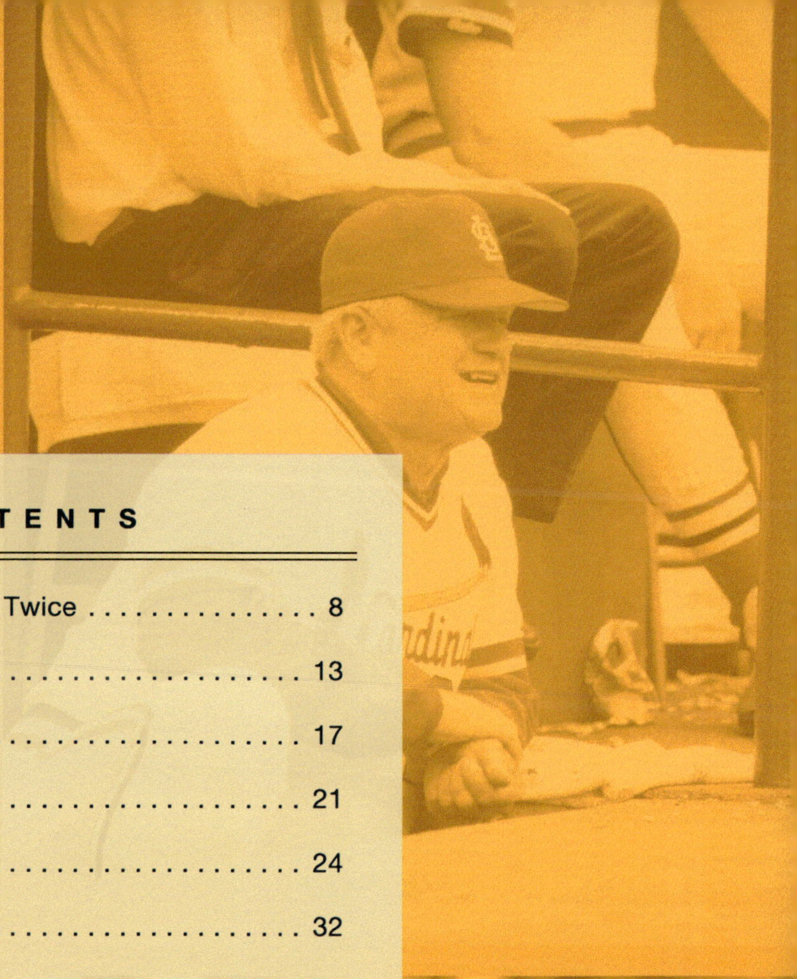

CONTENTS

EXTRA INNINGS

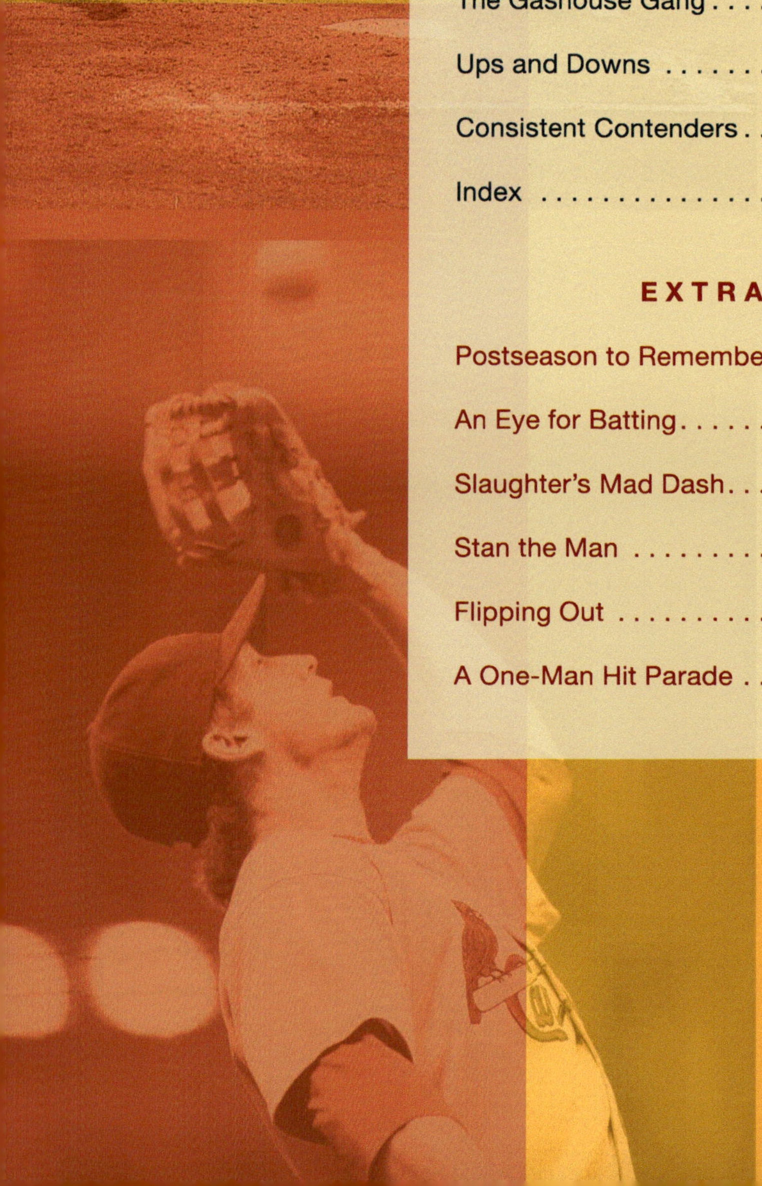

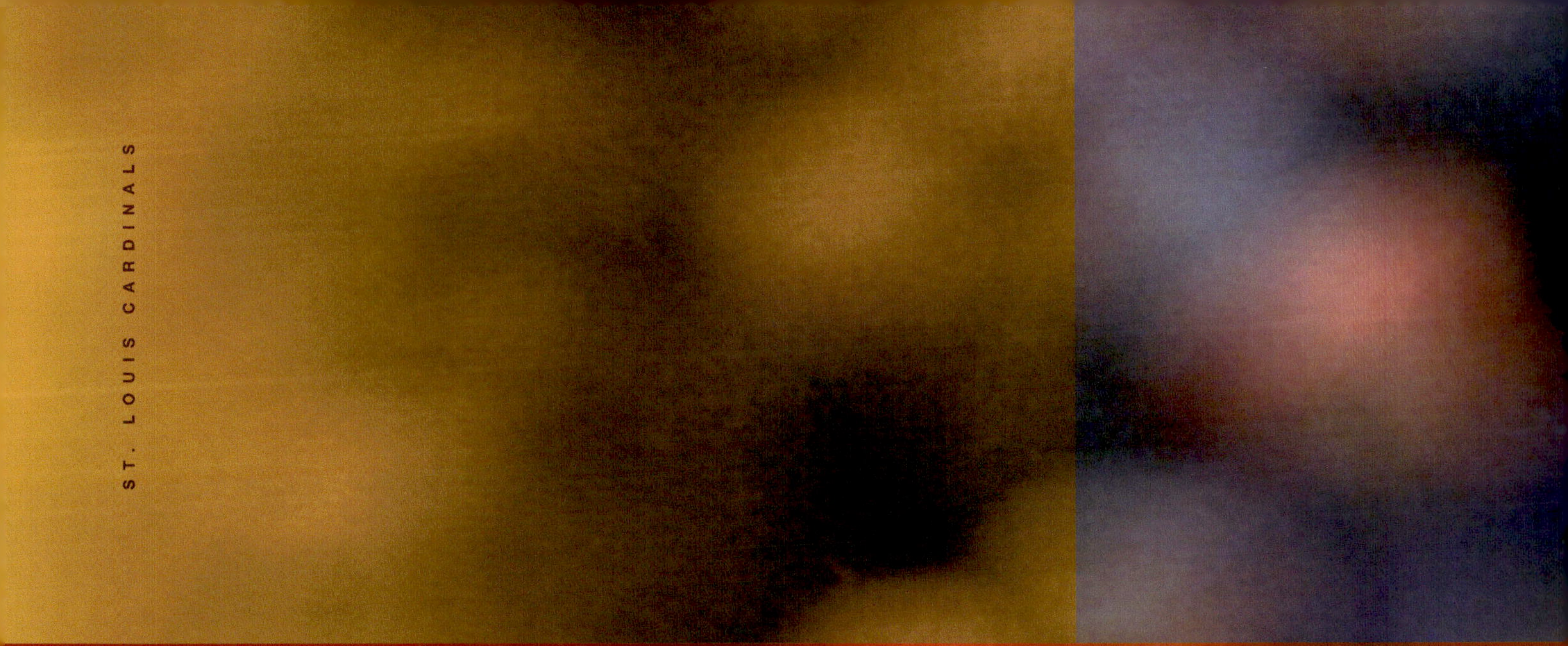

DOWN TO THE FINAL STRIKE... TWICE

The 2011 St. Louis Cardinals was a team that faced seemingly insurmountable odds. On August 24, the Los Angeles Dodgers completed a three-game sweep of the Cardinals in St. Louis. St. Louis' record was 67–63. It was 10 games behind the Milwaukee Brewers for first place in the National League (NL) Central Division. They were also 10.5 games behind the Atlanta Braves in the NL Wild Card standings. Cardinals manager Tony La Russa said about his team, "I guarantee that the team you have seen the past few weeks is not the team we have, and I believe you start to see our team tomorrow."

The next day, the Cardinals beat the Pittsburgh Pirates. They took three of four from Pittsburgh. The Cardinals continued to win in September. They went 18–8 in the season's final month. They were not able to catch Milwaukee for the division title. But they closed in on Atlanta for the wild card. The Cardinals and Braves were tied for the wild card going into the final game of the season. The Cardinals beat the Houston Astros, 8–0. Atlanta lost to the Philadelphia Phillies in extra innings. St. Louis had qualified for the playoffs.

Third baseman David Freese

EXTRA INNINGS

DAVID FREESE
THIRD BASEMAN
CARDINALS SEASONS: 2009–13
HEIGHT: 6-FOOT-2
WEIGHT: 213 POUNDS
KEY STATS: WORLD SERIES MVP, NLCS MVP, WORLD SERIES CHAMPION, 2012 ALL-STAR

POSTSEASON TO REMEMBER

David Freese grew up a fan of the St. Louis Cardinals. He was raised close to St. Louis in nearby Wildwood, Missouri. His heroics in the Cardinals' 2011 postseason run to the World Series will be remembered forever by St. Louis fans. In the NL Championship Series (NLCS) against Milwaukee, Freese batted .545 (12-for-22) with three home runs and nine runs batted in (RBI). St. Louis won the series in six games. Freese had eight hits in the World Series against Texas. His two hits in Game 6 will go down as two of the biggest, most clutch hits in MLB history. Freese was named Most Valuable Player (MVP) of both the NLCS and the World Series. He became the sixth player to win both awards in the same year.

St. Louis Skyline

St. Louis upset the Phillies and Brewers to claim the NL pennant. It faced the Texas Rangers in the World Series. The Cardinals trailed in the series 3 games to 2. Game 6 was played in St. Louis.

The game would be tied at 4–4 after six innings. Texas led off the seventh inning with back-to-back home runs from Adrian Beltre and Nelson Cruz. It added another run to take a 7–4 lead. The score stayed that way until the eighth. Cardinals left fielder Allen Craig hit a solo home run to pull St. Louis within a run at 7–5.

St. Louis still trailed by two runs going into the bottom of the ninth. Rangers' closer Neftalí Feliz came in to pitch. With one out Albert Pujols doubled. Lance Berkman followed with a walk. Craig struck out. Third baseman David Freese was the last hope for the Cardinals. He faced a 1–2 count. Texas was one strike away from winning their first World Series. Freese launched a ball deep to right field. It went over the head of Cruz, bounced off the wall, and rolled away from him. Both Pujols and Berkman scored to tie the game at 7–7. Freese slid into third base with a triple.

In the top of the 10th inning, Josh Hamilton hit a two-run home run for Texas. It took a 9–7 lead. The Cardinals cut it to 9–8 in the bottom of the

inning. Berkman was up with two outs. He faced a 2–2 count. Again, Texas was one strike away from winning the World Series. He lined a single to center to score Jon Jay from second base. The game was tied at 9–9.

The Rangers did not score in the top of the 11th inning. Freese led off the bottom half for St. Louis. He launched a 3–2 pitch deep over the center field wall. Remarkably, St. Louis won 10–9. FOX sports announcer Joe Buck said as the ball was going over the fence, "We will see you tomorrow night." His father, Jack, called the World Series for CBS Sports in 1991. He said the same words when Kirby Puckett of the Minnesota Twins hit a game-winning home run in Game 6. St. Louis won the next night 6–2 to win the World Series.

COMING OUT OF THE NEST

St. Louis's first professional baseball team was called the Brown Stockings. It began play in 1875. Following two National League (NL) seasons, the team folded in 1877. A new Brown Stockings team emerged in 1882. Soon renamed the St. Louis Browns, it joined the NL in 1892. It stumbled through seven losing seasons. The worst was 1897. The Browns won just 29 games. Brothers Frank and Stanley Robison bought the team two years later. They renamed it the Perfectos. They also replaced the players' drab brown stockings with bright red ones. Later that year, sportswriter Willie McHale overheard a fan remark that the new socks were "a lovely shade of cardinal." He used the name in his column. The new name stuck.

The Cardinals posted a 76–64 record in 1901. It would be 10 years before their next winning season. After several mostly lousy seasons, the Cardinals

1934 St. Louis Cardinals

won 87 games in 1921. Starting that year, second baseman Rogers Hornsby had an especially successful five-year stretch. During that time, his batting average was .402. He also drove in 598 runs (RBI).

Despite Hornsby's efforts, the Cardinals never finished higher than third. They finally broke out in 1926. It was Hornsby's second season as player/manager. On the first day of spring training, he called a team meeting. "If there's anybody in this room who doesn't think we're going to win the pennant," he said, "go upstairs and get your money and go home, because we don't want you around here." No one left. St. Louis won its first NL pennant that season. First baseman Jim Bottomley contributed a league-leading 120 RBI. Catcher Bob O'Farrell was named NL Most Valuable Player (MVP). A great defensive player, he also hit a robust .293.

The Cardinals split the first six games of the World Series with the New York Yankees. St. Louis took a 3–2 lead in Game 7. It lasted into the bottom of the ninth inning. With two outs, slow-footed Yankee slugger Babe Ruth tried to steal second. O'Farrell easily threw him out. St. Louis captured its first world championship.

The "Redbirds" traded Hornsby soon afterward. The move shocked the baseball world. Steady-hitting Frankie Frisch replaced him at second base. The Cardinals finished second in the NL. In 1928, St. Louis won the pennant. The World Series had little drama. The Yankees swept the Cardinals in four games.

EXTRA INNINGS

ROGERS HORNSBY
SECOND BASEMAN/MANAGER
CARDINALS SEASONS: 1915–26, 1933 (MANAGER, 1925–26)
HEIGHT: 5-FOOT-11
WEIGHT: 175 POUNDS
KEY STATS: 1942 HALL OF FAME INDUCTEE, 2X NL MVP, 7X BATTING CHAMPION, .358 CAREER BATTING AVERAGE

AN EYE FOR BATTING

Rogers Hornsby was noted for his keen eyesight. He did not read books or watch movies. He feared these activities would hurt his eyes. A young opposing pitcher once complained that the umpire was not calling strikes on Hornsby. “Son,” the umpire replied, “when you throw a strike, Mr. Hornsby will let you know.” Seven times, Hornsby led the league in batting. In 1924, he hit a remarkable .424. Since 1900, that is the highest single-season batting average in Major League Baseball (MLB). His .3585 career batting average is second only to Ty Cobb’s .3662 in MLB history (American and National League).

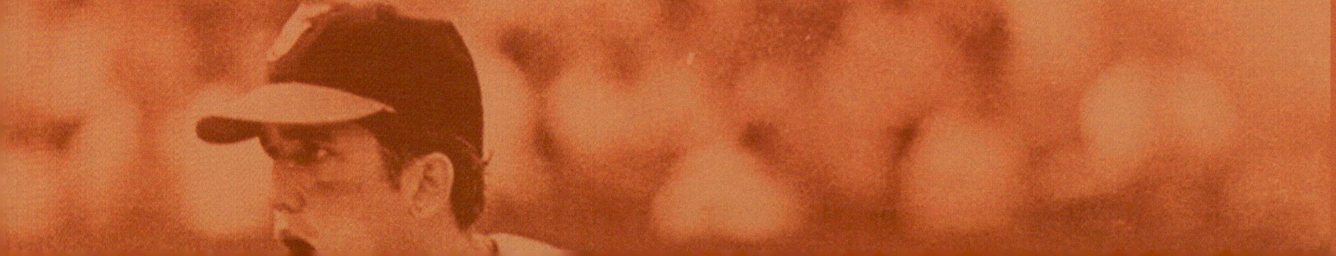

EXTRA INNINGS

ENOS SLAUGHTER
RIGHT FIELDER
CARDINALS SEASONS: 1938–42, 1946–53
HEIGHT: 5-FOOT-9
WEIGHT: 180 POUNDS
KEY STATS: 1985 HALL OF FAME INDUCTEE, 10X ALL-STAR, 4X WORLD SERIES CHAMPION, 1,304 CAREER RBI

SLAUGHTER'S MAD DASH

Enos Slaughter was not a man known for his speed. The most stolen bases he had in a season over his 19-year career was just nine. But there is one play where his speed helped give the Cardinals a World Series title. In Game 7 of the 1946 World Series, the Cardinals and Boston Red Sox were tied at 3–3 in the bottom of the eighth inning. Slaughter led off the inning with a single. The next two batters made outs. Slaughter remained at first base. Harry Walker came to the plate. A hit-and-run play was called. Slaughter took off with the pitch. Walker slapped a single to center field. Slaughter did not stop running. Boston players were stunned. Slaughter kept running around third base. The throw home was off-target. Slaughter scored. The Cardinals would win 4–3. The play became known as "Slaughter's Mad Dash."

THE GASHOUSE GANG

In 1930, the Cardinals captured the NL pennant again. They met the Philadelphia Athletics in the World Series. St. Louis lost in six games. The two teams clashed again in the World Series the following season. St. Louis took the series in seven games. Outfielder Pepper Martin led the Cardinals. He had 12 hits in 24 at-bats. He knocked in five runs and scored five more himself. He also stole four bases. "I did all right," the humble Martin said afterward.

Pitcher Dizzy Dean and left fielder Joe "Ducky" Medwick joined the team in 1932. Along with Frisch and Martin, they formed the heart of the "Gashouse Gang." This goofy group of Cardinals was known for its off-field antics and on-field wild play. But its talent was no joke. In 1934, the Gashouse Gang won the NL pennant. Dean won 30 games. His brother, rookie Paul Dean, notched 19 wins. Dizzy pitched a three-hit shutout in the first game of a late-season doubleheader. Paul tossed a no-hitter in the nightcap. The Cardinals faced the Detroit Tigers in the World Series. Before it began, Dizzy predicted that he and Paul would win two games apiece. They did. St. Louis captured its third championship.

The brother act was short-lived. Paul won 19 games again in 1935. Dizzy won 28. But Paul suffered a serious injury the following season. Then, in 1937, Dizzy was hit by a line drive. It broke his big toe. He returned to the mound before the injury healed, causing further damage. Neither Dean ever regained his dominant form. The gang, it seemed, had run out of gas.

The team continued to play reasonably well, though. In 1942, the Cardinals won 43 of their last 51 games. They edged out the Brooklyn Dodgers for the

Dizzy Dean, Frankie Frisch, Sam Breadon

pennant. The St. Louis team featured outfielders Enos Slaughter and Stan Musial. It also had smooth-fielding shortstop Marty Marion. Pitchers Johnny Beazley and MVP-winner Mort Cooper rounded out the roster. The Cardinals met the Yankees in the World Series. St. Louis lost Game 1. But it rallied. The team won the next four games to take the title.

Musial and Cooper led St. Louis to a second straight World Series showdown. Once again, the Cardinals faced the Yankees. This time, St. Louis was heavily favored. But New York prevailed. St. Louis won its third straight NL pennant in 1944. This time, the Redbirds faced their crosstown rival, the St. Louis Browns, in the World Series. The Cardinals won the "St. Louis Showdown" in six games.

In 1945, the Cardinals fell three games short of a fourth consecutive pennant. The following year, pitcher Howie Pollet led the NL with 21 wins. Second baseman Red Schoendienst was an All-Star. The NL featured another tight race between St. Louis and Brooklyn. The teams tied. St. Louis won a special tiebreaker series. It went on to beat the Boston Red Sox in the World Series.

Center fielder Jim Edmonds

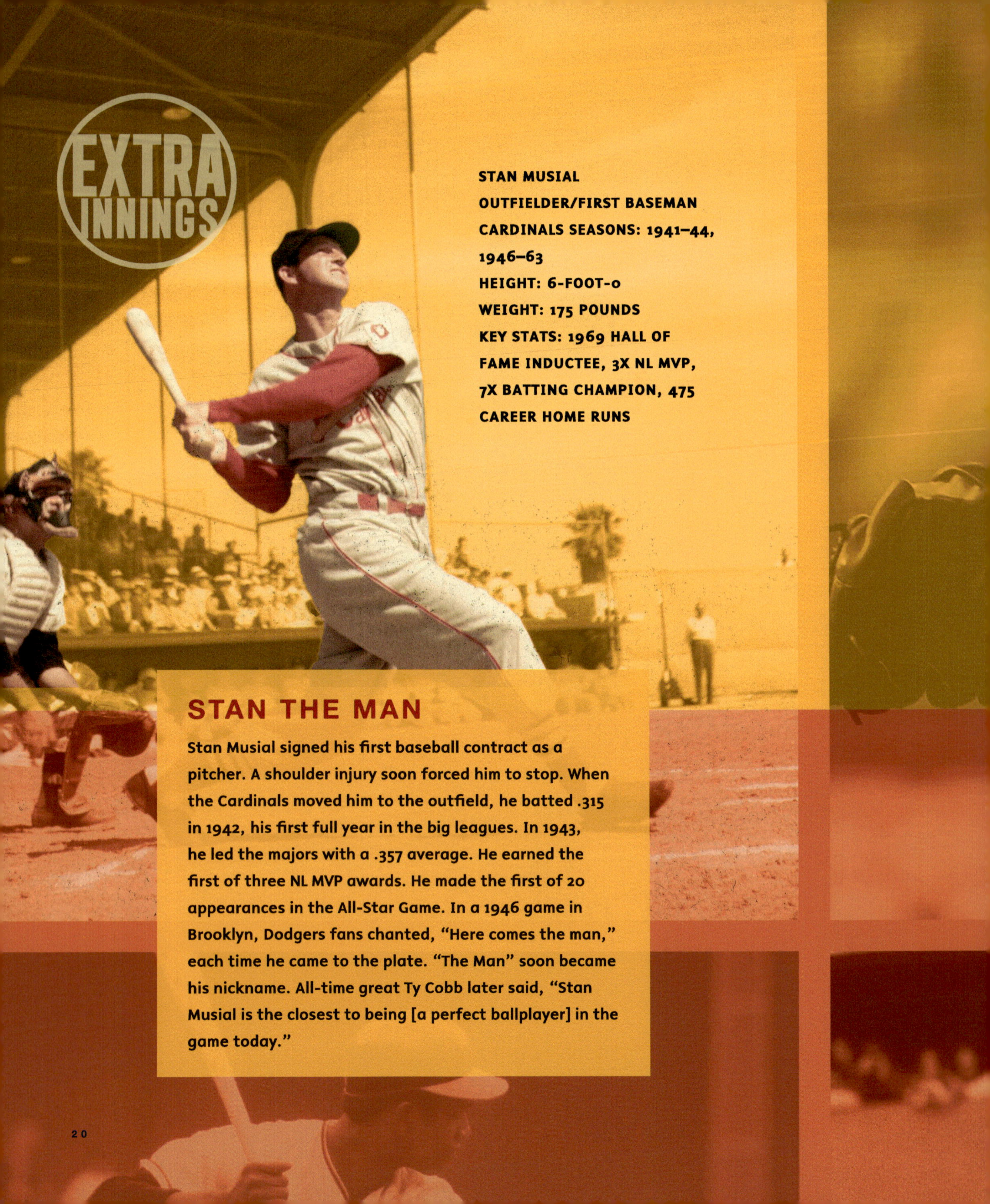

EXTRA INNINGS

STAN MUSIAL
OUTFIELDER/FIRST BASEMAN
CARDINALS SEASONS: 1941–44, 1946–63
HEIGHT: 6-FOOT-0
WEIGHT: 175 POUNDS
KEY STATS: 1969 HALL OF FAME INDUCTEE, 3X NL MVP, 7X BATTING CHAMPION, 475 CAREER HOME RUNS

STAN THE MAN

Stan Musial signed his first baseball contract as a pitcher. A shoulder injury soon forced him to stop. When the Cardinals moved him to the outfield, he batted .315 in 1942, his first full year in the big leagues. In 1943, he led the majors with a .357 average. He earned the first of three NL MVP awards. He made the first of 20 appearances in the All-Star Game. In a 1946 game in Brooklyn, Dodgers fans chanted, "Here comes the man," each time he came to the plate. "The Man" soon became his nickname. All-time great Ty Cobb later said, "Stan Musial is the closest to being [a perfect ballplayer] in the game today."

UPS AND DOWNS

The Cardinals finished second each year from 1947 to 1949. Then they began a long stretch of disappointment. Even as the team fell short, it featured talented players. Third baseman Ken Boyer, pitcher Bob Gibson, and catcher Tim McCarver played well in the late 1950s and '60s. Musial retired following the 1963 season. He was an All-Star in 20 of his 22 seasons with the team.

Speedy Lou Brock ignited the team. The left fielder's hitting and running helped turn things around. St. Louis regained its lofty status with another pennant 1964. It faced the Yankees in the World Series. The Cardinals won in seven games.

St. Louis was back in the World Series in 1967. It met Boston. Gibson had spent two months on the disabled list. He returned to pitch– and win– three complete games. He allowed only three total runs. The Cardinals won the series in seven games. Gibson was phenomenal in 1968. He had a minuscule earned run average (ERA) of 1.12. The Cardinals returned to the World Series. But they lost to the Tigers in seven games.

The league split into two divisions in 1969. St. Louis joined the NL East Division. The team struggled to climb higher than second in the division. A highlight came in 1974 when Brock stole an MLB record of 118 bases.

In 1982, the team hit only 67 home runs. Still, it won the pennant for the first time in 14 years. Outfielder Lonnie Smith stole 68 bases. Shortstop Ozzie Smith kept opposing players from scoring with his glove work. The Cardinals beat the Atlanta Braves in the NL Championship Series (NLCS). In the World

Outfielder Willie McGee

Series, St. Louis faced a bruising Milwaukee Brewers lineup. The Cardinals took the series in seven games. "There were a lot of people who just couldn't believe the Cardinals were world champions," said manager Whitey Herzog. "They seemed to think there was something wrong with the way we played baseball, with speed and defense and line-drive hitters."

St. Louis was back in the World Series in 1985 and 1987. It lost to the Kansas City Royals in an all-Missouri series in seven games in 1985. Two years later, the Cardinals lost to the Minnesota Twins in another seven-game series.

The early 1990s were tough for the Cardinals. They joined the new NL Central Division in 1994. Two years later, St. Louis ended a nine-year postseason drought. It climbed from nine games under .500 in May to win the division. The team swept the San Diego Padres in the NL Division Series (NLDS). But it lost to Atlanta in the NLCS.

Power-hitting first baseman Mark McGwire joined the team late in 1997. The following year, he hit an MLB-record 70 home runs. But St. Louis could not find its way back to the top. Still, as the 1990s ended, fans felt the team was ready to soar again.

CONSISTENT CONTENDERS

The Cardinals flew to the top of the NL Central in 2000. Center fielder Jim Edmonds hit 42 home runs and drove in 108 runs. St. Louis swept the Braves in the NLDS. But the New York Mets clipped the team's wings in the NLCS. The Cardinals picked up steam the following season. Rookie first baseman Albert Pujols took the league by storm. He batted .329 with 37

First baseman Albert Pujols

PUJOLS
5

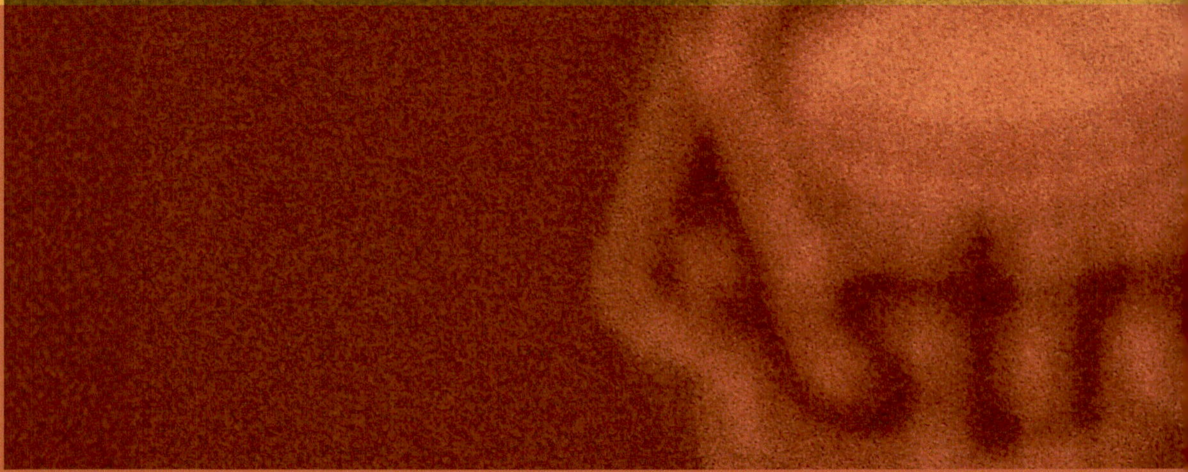

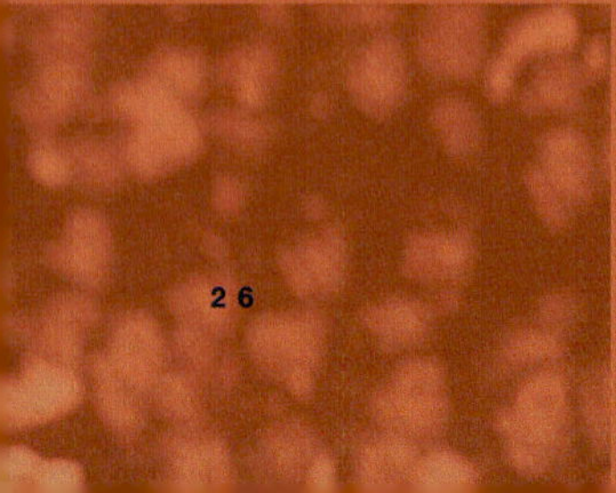

OZZIE SMITH
SHORTSTOP
CARDINALS SEASONS: 1982–96
HEIGHT: 5-FOOT-11
WEIGHT: 150 POUNDS
KEY STATS: 2002 HALL OF FAME INDUCTEE, 15X ALL-STAR, 13X GOLD GLOVE AWARDS, 2,460 CAREER HITS

FLIPPING OUT

Ozzie Smith was known for his gravity-defying athleticism. He did backflips at home games. He was nicknamed "The Wizard of Oz" for his magical fielding. He dove for ground balls seemingly destined to be base hits and often snagged them. Then he popped to his feet and threw out the batter as if such plays were routine. Manager Whitey Herzog claimed that Smith's defense saved 75 runs a year. He won 13 consecutive Gold Glove awards. Smith worked hard at offense, too. He progressed from being an easy out to winning the Silver Slugger award as the league's best-hitting shortstop in 1987.

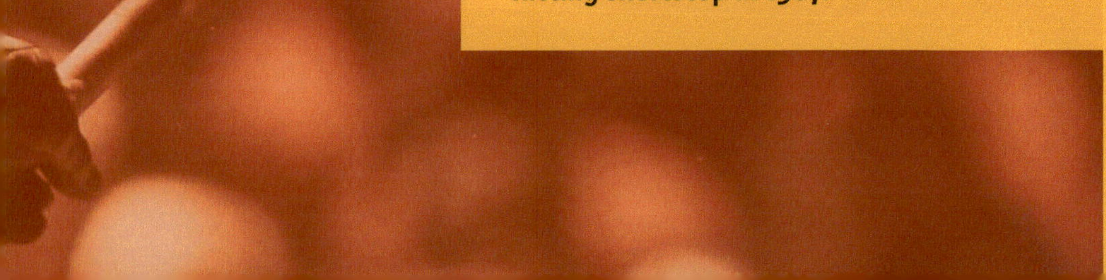

home runs and 130 RBI in his first big-league season. He was the easy choice for NL Rookie of the Year.

In 2004, the Cardinals won 105 games. Pitchers Jeff Suppan and Chris Carpenter piled up wins. Closer Jason Isringhausen slammed the door on opposing offenses. They met the red-hot Red Sox in the World Series. St. Louis got swept. The Redbirds maintained their first-place hold in the NL Central the following season. But the Houston Astros knocked them out in the NLCS.

The Cardinals won just 83 games in 2006. But it was still good enough to win the division. They went on a tear in the playoffs. St. Louis defeated the Padres in the NLDS. Then they beat the Mets in the NLCS. The Cardinals stomped the Tigers in five games to win the World Series. The 83 regular season wins are the worst for a World Series champion in MLB history.

St. Louis reached the playoffs just once over the next four seasons. Catcher Yadier Molina was a team leader. "El Capitan" won the first of nine Gold Glove awards in 2008. In 2010, ace pitcher Adam Wainwright won 20 games.

The team won 90 games in 2011. It reached the postseason as a Wild Card. Third baseman David Freese's magical postseason run guided St. Louis to an improbable 11th World Series title. The Cardinals had another unlikely postseason run the following year. They won 88 games and qualified as a Wild Card again. They topped Atlanta in the NL Wild Card Game (NLWC) and defeated the top-seeded Washington Nationals in the NLDS. In the NLCS, the Cardinals raced out to a 3–1 series lead against the San Francisco Giants. But the Giants won the final three games to claim the pennant.

The Cardinals won the division with 97 wins in 2013. They advanced to the World Series against Boston. St. Louis held a 2–1 series lead. But Boston won the next three to take the title. The Cardinals lost to the Giants, again, in the 2014 NLCS. St. Louis won 100 games in 2015. But it faced a hot Chicago Cubs team in the NLDS and lost in four games.

St. Louis missed the postseason the next three years. Molina continued to be a pillar behind the plate. He made his ninth All-Star appearance in 2019.

EXTRA INNINGS

ALBERT PUJOLS
FIRST BASEMAN
CARDINALS SEASONS: 2001–11, 2022
HEIGHT: 6-FOOT-3
WEIGHT: 235 POUNDS
KEY STATS: 3X NL MVP, 6X SILVER SLUGGER AWARD, 703 CAREER HOME RUNS, 2X WORLD SERIES CHAMPION

A ONE-MAN HIT PARADE

Albert Pujols's talent was not immediately obvious to MLB scouts. The Cardinals finally took him in the 13th round in the 1999 MLB Draft. It was one of their best moves ever. He was NL Rookie of the Year in 2001. He batted .329, slammed 37 home runs, and drove in 130 runs. He kept getting better. He was a combination of power and contact hitting. He won the batting title in 2003. Twice he led the NL in home runs. He also won two Gold Glove awards. Pujols was named MVP three times and runner-up four more times. He returned to play his final big-league season in St. Louis. In 2022, he became the fourth player in MLB history to hit 700 career home runs.

St Louis
33

Pitcher Andre Pallante

After a midseason slip, the Cardinals rallied to win the NL Central. They faced Atlanta in the NLDS. The teams split the first four games. In the first inning of the decisive Game 5, St. Louis exploded for 10 runs. That was the biggest opening inning in MLB playoff history. The Cardinals won 13–1. That sent them to the NLCS. But they were swept by Washington.

The 2019 season was the first of four straight playoff appearances. But the last three years were met with quick exits. In the COVID-shortened 2020 season, the team finished just two games over .500. It lost to San Diego in the NLWC series. They lost in the Wild Card round the next two seasons as well.

The years saw additions of great players. First baseman Paul Goldschmidt arrived in 2019. He was named NL MVP in 2022 after hitting 35 home runs and driving in 115 runs. Third baseman Nolan Arenado came in 2021. He made three straight All-Star appearances.

St. Louis won just 71 games in 2023. It marked their lowest win total in a full MLB season since 1990. It bounced back to 83 wins in 2024. But it missed the playoffs.

The Cardinals boast one of the proudest histories in Major League Baseball. As of 2024, their 11 World Series trophies are second most in MLB history. The team posted only two losing seasons since 2000. It should be no surprise that the Redbirds plan to fly away with another world championship soon.

Second baseman Brendan Donovan

INDEX